Native Echoes

Listening to the Spirit of the Land

Also by the Author

Chief Joseph and the Flight of the Nez Perce
Make Me an Instrument of Your Peace
Neither Wolf nor Dog
The Wolf at Twilight
The Girl who Sang to the Buffalo
Voices in the Stones
Letters to my Son
Small Graces

Cover and Text Design: Hok - Michael Hawkins / MindCanvas.com
Front Cover Photo: Erik J. Fremstad

Native Echoes was previously published in substantially similar form as *A Haunting Reverence* by New World Library (1996) and University of Minnesota Press (1999). Endorsement quotes are from those editions.

Cover photo, "Giving up the Dead" by Erik J. Fremstad.
www.erikfremstad.com / Facebook: Fine art by Erik Fremstad.

Wolf nor Dog
Books

Native Echoes

Listening to the Spirit of the Land

For the children,
that they may learn early
what we must hope
that we have not learned too late.

Twenty years ago, during the coldest winter in recent memory, I embarked upon a literary journey to give voice to the spirit of the land that I called my home.

This book – *Native Echoes: Listening to the Spirit of the Land* – was the result of that journey. It was my homage to the power of the great natural forces that surround us and shape our hearts and spirits, and a bowing before the spiritual insights of the Native people with whom I lived and worked. I loved it as my "quiet child."

Though *Native Echoes* found its inspiration in the land of the north, the same book could as easily be written about the spiritual power of the sun-blessed American Southwest, or the great haunting distances of the Alaskan interior, or the rolling hills and whispering forests of Appalachia and the Piedmont. For *Echoes* is not about a particular place, it is about the very power of place itself. It is about listening to the land, and learning the lessons she has to teach.

Over the years I have often revisited this quiet work for inspiration, and to remind myself of the power of metaphor to shape a truth that cannot easily be contained in description and narration. *Native Echoes* was just that – pure metaphor — a painting in words in search of the living, breathing, presence of the land.

But it was more, as well. It was an attempt to meld the richness and insight of our western spiritual tradition with the Native heartbeat of our American land – a search, if you will, for an authentic American spirituality.

All writers, indeed, all artists, know that there are times when you catch something in passing that you will never catch again. Years later, when you go back to that work, you stare at it with amazement, wondering how you managed to capture that moment and give it a form that seems so irreducible and right.

Native Echoes, which was originally published as *A Haunting Reverence*, is such a work. I am filled with gratitude and humility that I was able to give it birth.

I believe it is time for *Native Echoes* to be heard again. In a world that seeks spirituality without dogma, where there is hunger to learn the teachings of the land, it offers gentle guidance and quiet reflection.

I hope you will give yourself over to this work. If you still your mind and quiet your heart, it will reward you. It speaks to many spiritual questions in the only way that such questions can be addressed — as poetry, as metaphor, as a grasping at a shaft of light.

Kent Nerburn
Minnesota and Oregon 2016

The White man does not
understand America. He is too far removed
from its formative processes. The roots of the tree
of his life have not yet grasped the rock and the soil. . .
Men must be born and reborn to belong. Their bodies
must be formed of the dust of their
forefathers' bones.

— Chief Luther Standing Bear
Lakota

When you till the ground, it shall no longer yield to you its strength;
you shall be a fugitive and a wanderer on the earth.

— The book of Exodus, chapter 4, verse 12

CONTENTS

Kent Nerburn

PROLOGUE

We are as children on this land, a shadow on the still life of time.

We measure our presence in generations; we cannot dig down ten thousand years and find our bones.

Our arrival is scribed upon the line of history; it does not drift upon the winds of story, or float upon the shrouds of myth.

We are explorers and discoverers still, seeking meaning through movement and examination.

But we are coming to a time of listening. Our sweat and breath are now upon this land.

Voices rise up, and we begin to hear the echoes in the stones.

The calm dignity of a rock.

The fleeting fairness of a summer field.

A mountain, indifferent and impenetrable, thrusting

through the clouds. They claim us and inhabit us.

By the distance of their horizons they shape our

dreams, and by the care with which they receive our

footsteps they form our hearts.

Theophany? Is that too strong a word?

To hear the voice of God within the land?

There are prayerfields in our reveries, and we must

wander until we find them.

Whisperings

And when your children's children think themselves alone in the field, the store, the shop, upon the highway, or in the silence of the pathless woods, they will not be alone.

— Chief Seattle
Suquamish/Duwamish

BURIAL

We do not own the land. We belong to it. And by our sweat and breath shall
she know us, and welcome us upon our return.
— Pueblo saying

I am standing before a northern lake on a windswept point of land as a young Indian boy I know is lowered into the earth by his friends and family. It is a strange and lonely funeral — they all are in their own way. But this boy was a friend of mine, and his loss has struck me with unusual force.

He was a quiet sort who kept his counsel except to joke occasionally when joshed or teased. He had been a boxer, a good one, but had given it up, and had taken, as his grandmother told me, to staying up all night and lifting weights at three in the morning.

He drank, would not talk to her, became sullen and distant. So great was his mask that soon all chose to ignore him. But, as with all hidden faces, his shone with a special grace when in those unguarded moments it opened with a warm and honest smile.

These smiles are what I remember most about him.

The funeral was typical of his native community. Babies cried. People smoked cigarettes. The coffin stood in the center of a dingy community gym, while people sat around the outside edges on bleachers, like spectators at a basketball game. The family and friends — honored guests and deepest mourners — were on folding chairs facing the casket.

One part of the gym was given over to a potluck, and each person stopped briefly and scraped a bit of food into a box to be placed before the grave so the departing spirit could have nourishment on its journey to the afterlife. The head man of the community, who was also the spiritual leader, spoke only briefly in English before turning to Ojibwe.

Young girls sobbed. Young men stared at the ceiling. As the words were finished, the door to the outside was pushed opened and the casket was wheeled forward into the shaft of intruding daylight. The head man shook a rattle and chanted a low mournful prayer that sounded almost like a lullaby. A circle of men began drumming and singing.

Amidst much grunting and shouted direction, the casket was wrestled out through the door and onto the bed of a waiting pickup truck to be carried to the lonely promontory where the boy would be laid to rest among his ancestors.

The wind was warm. The sky was an empty blue. Leaves had fallen, but the memory of summer warmth was everywhere.

It was a good day to die.

I have lived, now, for years in this northwestern part of Minnesota, this forgotten corner of our country, where the prairies meet the woodlands, the Mississippi starts its course, and the water changes flow from south to north.

This is not a gentle place, but neither is it heroic. It is ruminative, reflective, a land of changes, where one cannot believe too strongly in the joys of summer or the trials of winter, because the turning of the seasons is ever present in the mind.

It is a land of harsh realities. Settlers who stopped in this place were unable to find an easy rest. They chose here because they were the outlaws, the misfits, the desperately poor, or those who had to rage and measure themselves against some brutal but indifferent god.

Men became suspicious; women became depressed. The earth gave but little, and what it gave came grudgingly. Rocks pushed like cruel jokes through the impoverished soil, and mocked the efforts of the farmers to bring forth crops from the sun-starved ground.

This was not my native home. I was born further to the south, though not by much. But my childhood was lived under spreading trees, not among the darkness of the pines. To come to this more northern land was to discover something new, more brooding, deeper, almost sinister.

It was a life of contrasts: dark forests, bright lakes; harsh winters, indolent summers. People huddled close to the earth, and lived their lives in frenzied spasms of activity when for a few short months the sunfall days blew dappled through the summer pines.

Death was a way of life here, from gunshot, from freezing, from wandering off in the middle of winter, from despair. People killed to live, and they lived to kill. Hunting was religion; fishing, worshipful sport. In the fall, deer carcasses hung from tripods made of logs. Stringers of fish were displayed proudly and young boys were told that in their skill at killing lay their claim to manhood.

It repelled me, and it fascinated me.

There was an elemental grandeur somewhere in this way of living, but it was submerged under brutishness, and too often celebrated for its squalid resistance to anything ennobling or full of grace.

Greatness had no shape beyond the number of trees that could be sheared from the land, or the profusion of pelts that could be hung from a pole. Courage was embodied in the logger who dragged himself five miles through the forest and the snow after accidentally severing his own leg with a chainsaw.

Civilization was under siege, or, at best, present in its most rudimentary form. Often I have wanted to escape.

But civilization is a malleable concept. Other voices speak as well.

This is also Indian land. Its marshy surfaces and low-lying, scrubby cover made it rich in bounty for those who hunted and gathered as a way of life. And its stolid resistance to tilling has kept the full force of white settlement away. Even now the reservations surround the towns and serve as ghostly reminders that we who have come from other shores are still but visitors here, understanding only dimly the ways of the land that we have appeared to conquer.

In the Indians who have made their home here — like my young departed friend — something lives that invests this harsh land with spiritual value.

It is not some romantic taproot into primeval forest mysteries and pre-Adamic unities with nature. It is far more integrated, far more resolved and inseparable from their character. Their furtiveness fits perfectly with the dark corners of the forest. Their judgmental ways are in keeping with the demanding indifference of the land. Their silence suits the distances; their way of thinking meanders like the trails on the hillsides and the oxbows in the creeks. In their fatalism one senses the turning of the seasons, a peaceful acquiescence devoid of pessimism and despair.

It is akin to a Taoist understanding, but with a darker musk, where nature is not merely the reflection of a life well-lived, but is the very crucible from which all understanding comes. Animals are teachers, the landscape shapes personal psychology, and the dominant natural forces are the point of contact with deity and the template of spiritual understanding.

Far from seeming brutish, the native people seemed grounded and resolved, and their lack of civilization felt more like an integration into nature than a failure to conquer its rough forms.

Kent Nerburn

Several years ago, the boy laid out before me was part of a group that I brought to visit the man who now stands over him giving the final benediction. It was an organized attempt to bring the voice of the elders to the ears of the youth. The elder spoke of the traditional ways of teaching; how an infant was carried on the back, facing out, so it might see where the mother has been, and thus gain the knowledge of the mother's daily life; how the hands were swaddled, so the child must learn stillness and how to observe; how the infant was placed upright, beneath a tree, so it would have, as its constant companion, the movements of the wind.

He told them of the animals, of how the bear was observed in order to see which plants were safe to eat, how the wolf was taken as the model of fidelity, and how the eagle was studied for its ways of raising the young.

The young people fidgeted and stared. They whispered to each other. The old man was going on too long.

Like an animal going back into the forest, he closed his eyes, turned inward, and was gone.

We have on this land a clash of genius. The European, logical heir to the Greeks, the Romans, the Christian in all its forms, brought to these shores a faith in progress, a teleology of hope. It is a fine and noble instinct, too quickly denigrated these days, that finds truth in movement, in discovery, in examination, in a promise of perfectibility. It is the motive force of evolution, the engine of exploration, the philosophical extrapolation of the way we experience time.

Yet there are other ways. The cyclical, the circular, the great gyre of repetitive ritual is also written in the earth in which we live. The planets, wheeling though time, the seasons, repeating their eternal liturgy, speak of a past that is always alive in the present, and an earth revealed by ever more acute understanding of analogy.

The mandala and the medicine wheel, as surely as the quest for the grail, reveal a path of spiritual understanding.

My young friend was caught in between. His progress had been too slow; his faith in the eternal lessons of nature too weak a balm. He had lived his life suspended between truths, and in the end, neither had been strong enough to save him.

He is being buried in his traditional garb. His face is painted; he is wearing feathers. Loving, grieving hands have laid him out, dressed him, and prepared him in the traditional way, far from antiseptic funeral parlors and stainless steel gurneys and bottles of fluids. He is being sent off with rattles and chants that he only dimly understood, to an afterlife in which he only half-believed.

These are not easy days. We stumble on the foundations of our faith. Our belief in the rational demands first principles, from which all must logically evolve. Yet our need for life is so strong, our faith in Being so immutable, that we want creators, intercessors, presences in our lives.

We want our belief inhabited by logic, but we also want it infused with life and personal contact, and, lacking both, we cry out like the desperate man in the Gospels, "I believe, I believe. Help my unbelief."

They are placing him in the earth now. The hole is not squared. It was dug by friendly hands, not by those who make a business of interment. They lower the casket on rope slings; if they let one slip, he will spill out. People sit on hoods of cars, smoking cigarettes, waiting. The birds fly overhead. So large a gathering makes them curious. Perhaps they sense the presence of death.

Kent Nerburn

Beneath our days, beneath our community, beneath even our culture and our history, lies a layer of meaning. It has a logic, and it has a life. It pivots on the movements of the stars and pulsates with the drumbeat of the seasons. Here thunder shapes the voice of God, the birds reveal the ways of motherhood. Plants scream when pulled, and flourish when exposed to song. Our strength reflects what the landscape demands; rocks reveal the shape of protection. The spirits of our fathers put a face upon our courage and bears teach men to dance. Life is lived in a symphony of revelation, and children learn to fear the shadow or to celebrate the light.

The boy is in the earth, now. We walk up, one by one, and shovel a mound of dirt into the hole. It echoes hard and hollow on the casket. The young men — his friends — jump in the hole and pack soil around the sides. They are forceful, abrupt, alive with the importance of their task.

The old man steps to the side of the grave. He lights the pipe, offers smoke in the four directions, toward mother earth, toward father sky. He speaks, low, in Ojibwe. I recognize the word for bear, the word for eagle. The others' heads are bowed, as they are at all places, in all times, in the presence of death.

The old man places the tobacco, the sacred herb, in the grave. It comes from the earth, it rises to the heavens. It follows all laws of those who would return to God.

We cannot find our lives in weights and measures.

Microscopes and telescopes increase our context; they do not find origins or conclusions. Like the spirit we brought to this land, they probe, they examine, they explore. "Meaning," they proclaim, "is beyond our vision.

Truth is below our sight."

But there is research of a different sort. It does not move, it does not seek. It watches until stillness shifts or silence makes a sound. It drinks in a universe whose origin and every manifestation is alive, and whose every movement demonstrates its laws. That which exists beyond our boundaries is not unknown, it simply is not revealed.

A final prayer is offered. The young men shape the earth into a mound above the grave — the geometry of folded hands, of pyramids, of pines.

I turn and walk away. For me, it is finished. To stay longer would be false and intrusive, an arrogance uncalled for by the moment. What remains is hidden, closed to me by the barriers of culture. My presence here has been enough.

I walk toward the waning sun. I turn once toward the east, toward the secrecy of the forests, once toward the west, where the prairies come alive with autumn light. I turn south to where the Mississippi starts the passage that clefts the bosom of this land, and to the north, where the waters beneath us flow together and commingle with the Arctic seas.

Behind me I hear the drumming and the mournful wail of the singers offering up their final song.

It is good, I tell myself, to live in this land of transitions, this land incipient with change, where the heart is drawn always beyond itself, and every ending is numinous with hope.

Kent Nerburn

A MEMORY
OF TREES

"I see men; but they look like trees, walking."
—A blind man, partially healed
by Jesus, in the 8th chapter of
The Gospel of Mark

The days of my childhood were spent beneath two favorite trees. One, a grand maple, grew in our neighbor's back yard. Its first branch, one boost by a friend above the ground, was a massive arm that extended sideways on the horizontal for several feet before turning directly upward, like a weightlifter showing off his bicep. This arm was a cherished sanctuary for us all. Sufficiently above the ground to be free from the earth, it nonetheless accepted us with all the graciousness of a summer meadow. We could sit three abreast on its ample breadth, and dream the dreams of a childhood unfettered by earthly concerns. When it was time to leave, there was just enough distance to the ground to offer us an instant of the exhilarating panic of freefall.

We would land, become earthbound, and run to the houses to answer the calls of our mothers, becoming once again the sons and the daughters and little people for whom life was a series of tiny obligations in a world we barely understood.

Sometimes, when the wind was strong, I would sneak out and climb onto the arm of the maple, just to feel its strength as the branches lashed and writhed above me. The tree would creak and groan in the surging wind, but the branch would never move. I held tight to it as the turbulence raged about me, secure in its strength, and buoyed by a confidence that was greater than my fear.

Then there was the pussywillow. It grew in our front yard and spread its arms in all directions like the arcs of falling stars. Perhaps it was a variety uncommon in our area. Perhaps it had managed to rise from the lowly condition of bush through some miraculous conjunction of nutrients and circumstance. But, without doubt, it was a tree.

Unlike the maple, we could easily step into the crook of the pussywillow. It, too, had a first branch. But hers — we always assumed she was a woman — was more a forking than a branching. One boy could rest comfortably in this fork; it was a template for a laconic slouch, like the poses boys took against a schoolyard wall.

The pussywillow was not a sanctuary. She was too public. She was the gathering place — "meet you at the pussywillow" — the place of planning. She was also the benefactor, and for that she suffered greatly.

Each year, when she would bloom, I would take a sprig of pussywillows to my teachers. It was a common ritual to bring flowers from our yards — lilacs, a tulip, whatever offered fragrance and color to the drabness of our schoolday life. It was always mine to bring the pussywillows; they were rare and unusual and had a hint of the excitement of a living animal, with their soft furry buds that everyone wanted to touch.

To bring them made me feel superior, above the ordinary, a youthful Balthazar bearing a gift far beyond the simple tributes of daisies and pansies that came from other children's hands.

But always, the teacher balked. "There is no such thing as a pussywillow tree," she would say.

I would protest. She would correct me. "Pussywillows grow on

Kent Nerburn

bushes, not on trees."

Invariably I would find myself under attack, either for my honesty or my accuracy. The gift borne with such a sense of childhood nobility would become a test of my character.

Still, I persisted. It was not for me that I did this: I knew the result. It was for the tree. In some corner of my childhood dreams I knew that our pussywillow was special, and had to mean more than just a meeting place for boys embarking on childhood adventures. In her was embodied some aesthetic impulse, some altruism, some gentility that I could not articulate but desperately wanted to express.

"Yes, there are pussywillow trees," I would say. "We have one in our front yard."

Sometimes, if the confrontation became intense, my mother would become involved, sending notes attesting to the veracity of my story. Such notes were dealt with like all parental notes: they ended the issue in terms of my involvement. It was now being adjudicated in a higher court, and neither my protests nor my concerns were any longer relevant.

One year, a teacher even drove by our house to see if there really was a pussywillow tree. The next day she affirmed my story. But the damage had been done. Our pussywillow had been reduced from a delicate and beautiful giver of gifts to the central object in a discussion of botany or ethics. The tree I loved had been made into a cipher in larger intellectual issues. Her ineffable gentleness had been forgotten, her silent softness ignored.

One day, I came home to find her gone. My father had chopped her down. The mindless picking of boys at her bark, the endless climbings and swingings and snapping of branches to make whips and gifts had taken their toll. In our love for her we had killed her.

I ran in panic from the jagged stump, and found her in a pile in our backyard. My father was bent over her, feeding chunks and cuttings into an angry, swirling fire that rose like a pyre from a corner of the yard.

I stood quietly behind him, watching his powerful arms, as he threw her limb by limb into the hungry flames. Helpless, I ran to the maple and hoisted myself onto the protection of its great branch. The smoke from the fire rose, shifted, and sought me out. The coals stared up at me with animals' eyes.

Long into the dark I sat there, silent among the foliage, ignoring my parents' calls and pleadings. I could see them moving below me, combing the shadows for their lost son. But I would not answer. They looked like trees walking, and I was choked with an unknown grief.

Kent Nerburn

Kent Nerburn

SILENT CITY

Of the wind only
Am I afraid.
—Ojibwe song

There is a place, not far from my home, that the Indians call Silent City.

It is just a field, no different than so many others, dotted with the occasional oak and covered in summer with nondescript dun grasses. In the winter, snow drifts across it with democratic impunity. Even it can find no reason to stop here.

But someone did stop here. In this field, so carefully carried in memory by the Ojibwe, two groups of men surprised each other. The one, Ojibwe, was seeking room to live and hunt as their people were pushed deeper into the woodlands by the coming of the European. The other, Sioux, was struggling to retain a foothold in the woodlands as they were pushed ever and further into the treeless prairies to the west.

Here, in this field, too sparse to be called woods, too ordinary to be called prairie, they met, and fought. The Ojibwe, more conversant with the whites, had procured more guns. The Sioux, perhaps sensing that their destiny was in the open west, were fighting in retreat. All the forces, save bravery and honor, weighed in favor of the Ojibwe, and the outcome, save for bravery and honor, went their way.

As the battle closed, so memory goes, in this field lay slain one hundred Sioux warriors. Young men dying to protect their families; old men dying to protect their honor; killed by arrow, bullet, and cudgel; dying quickly, dying slowly. Dying far from their families and far from history. Committing their spirits to the soil. To the field. To Silent City.

Now, the Ojibwe say, there are the voices. Here, on this desolate part of their land, so sparsely settled that one goes for miles on gravel roads to even find a house—here, where water lives so close to the surface that the rains can turn the field to swamp—here, where life is so spare that only the small and scuttling of the animal people can survive—the voices can be heard. Crying. Screaming. Moaning. Speaking not the language of the Ojibwe, but the language of the Sioux.

Who is to say how one claims the land? To plot, to measure, to till? To pay in coin or in blood? To trod the land for a thousand years, to bury our parents and our children upon it? None of these will guarantee our claim. It is for the land, and the land alone, to decide.

Somewhere, miles from here, standing lonely on a windswept Dakota prairie, a woman lifts her heart and cries her grandfather's name.

Somewhere, close to here, in a treeless, barren field, two boys stop their play and hear a moaning in the wind.

Kent Nerburn

Kent Nerburn

MADONNA OF THE ROCKS

The rocks are ringing,
The rocks are ringing.

— Paiute ghost dance song

It lay among a river of rocks. It may have been there for ten thousand years. That is what bothers me, that it may have been there for ten thousand years. I was a sculptor once, and you must know these things.

We had crossed the Yukon River hours or days ago, I do not remember now. And then the Arctic Circle.

To the eye expecting the exotic it was disappointing — still trees, rocks, mountains. But the heartbeat was different, and had been getting different for days. The earth was tilted, the sun came at us from an unknown angle.

I don't know why we were stopped. I don't remember if there were mountains or not. I don't remember anything except the river of rocks, the millions of rocks, and I was walking among them. It was a torrent of stones, this great running hollow of rocks, the memory of a flood, an echo of water madrush escaping from the glacier.

It was so fresh and yet so ancient. It thundered with remembered movement, but there was no history, no footprint upon the land. Earth forces roared beneath me, while the sky above was holy silence.

I could hear these rocks. They were singing, clattering. It was a clucking, like tenpins being knocked together. It was the sound of millions, until it became a cosmic laughter, or a call. It was outside, it was inside. I heard it in my head until I thought I was insane.

I covered my ears, but that only made it louder. I wanted to laugh. I did laugh, or maybe I shouted.

I walked. The stones laughed and clucked together. The remembered water roared beneath me. The remembered glacier groaned and sang. In some place I did not see, a multitude of seabirds lifted off and beat their wings. The wind blew from the edge of time.

Then I saw it.

I remember how it was: "Oh," I said. That was all. Not, "Eureka!" Not a gasp. Not, "Dear God." Just, "Oh."

It was not a discovery, it was a completion.

I reached down and picked her up. The curve of her back fit in my hand. My fingers slid gently into the place where her arm gave way to her hip. As my hand curved around her, my thumb slipped into the hollow where the child pressed his head against her.

She fit my hand like a weapon, or a gift.

I looked at her, and I stopped. The torrent stopped. The clucking stopped.

You must understand this: she was only a rock; a rock, from among millions. She had not been worked, not been touched. She had been chunked off an ancient mountain, ground by ice to a boulder, then to a stone, washed round by some ancient cataract, and left. She had been there for ten thousand years. She was a rock, and she had known no contact with the human.

There is a story — we have all heard it — about the woman who was sitting on a bench when the bomb exploded over Hiroshima, about how she was atomized, vaporized, immolated to cosmic dust in an instant, but how her

Kent Nerburn

shadow was burned onto a wall, and remains.

Michelangelo said that if you labor in good heart for all your life, once before you die you may come upon a single image strong and true.

I cradled her in my hand. She held her child close, as if protecting him from me. The child pressed against her, dissolving into her, like some weathered madonna of Giovanni Pisano, or a mother and child by Henry Moore.

Her back was smooth where she touched my flesh. Her front, where she held the child, was scrilled and striated by the ancient washings of stones and sand. She was hard, unbelievably hard, and grey as the dawn of time.

Ten years before, I had stood on the edge of Hudson Bay looking out over the sea of stones and boulders strewn across the margins of the shore by the glacier. This was the Pre-Cambrian shield, the oldest rocks on earth, scraped and revealed by the grinding of a mile-high wall of ice. Some had been left on end. They stood like ancient dolmens in the fading arctic light.

I remembered reading of the Inuit sculptors, who held their rocks in their hand as they worked, and how they sang to their stones to make the image come out. Who had made the Venus of Willendorf, and why? The cave paintings at Lascaux?

I cradled her in my hand, unwilling to let her go.

The clucking began again. I would not put her down. It became louder, like rainfall.

I turned and ran back to the truck. The others had not yet returned. I dug into my pack and found a towel and wrapped her in it.

The rocks were clucking from the draw.

I climbed inside the truck. I remembered reading that lightning could not strike you in a car because the tires disconnected you from the earth.

When the others returned we drove away. I told no one.

Now she is mine. She is cold even when it is warm. She lies on my mantle resting on her side. I do not know what to do. When I die, if she is buried with me, the world loses her. If she is not, she will be discarded, here on the ground thousands of miles from her home.

I pray often. I fear the sound of rocks. I have not sculpted again.

I tell my friends she is just a stone I found in the Arctic.

They need know nothing more.

Herod might be among us.

Kent Nerburn

Each road, a tributary, feeding the river of our life,

A metaphor of meaning written in the land.

A sound, a cast of light,

A conversation in passing,

And we are changed.

"The trail is beautiful," say the Navajo. "Be still."

The trail is beautiful. Be still.

Wanderings

*When you see a new trail, or a footprint you
do not know, follow it to the point of knowing.*

— Uncheedah
Santee Sioux

OLD ROADS, ANCIENT PATHWAYS

Give us many good roads
— Quiche' prayer

The trail winds, small and narrow, through the woods near my home. It passes along the margins of our lake. There is something of the patrol about it; it does not meander and stop at interesting points, and only seldom makes its way directly to the water's edge. The work of deer, perhaps, or a dog intent upon efficient survey of the land he claims for his own

I have seen such trails a thousand times — in the Bear's Paw mountains of Montana, the desiccated creek beds of the Badlands — anywhere that passage required care and forethought. They contain the accumulated wisdom of generations, of humans and animals working in common purpose, marking with their footfalls the choices that prudent transit required.

It is in such trails that we feel the heartbeat of our land. They are the capillaries of intention, marking the way for larger passages yet to come.

And when those passages arrive, becoming arteries of commerce and movement, it is good to look back and try to remember the trails that gave them birth.

Often, while on a road or highway, I try to see through the veil of time, to imagine the trail behind the route I am following. On occasion a roadside marker will reveal some tale about a pioneer passage, or mark some event that caused the road to pass by this point.

But go back further still. Why was this route chosen at all? What Native person, unacquainted with even the horse, first marked it out as a reasonable passage?

And even further, what animal had first staked its claim upon this route, and to what end? When we can no longer see the trails behind the roads, our lives are getting dangerously far from the heartbeat of the land.

This is why the railroad holds so much peace for those of us who love it. In its desperate attempt to bridge the continent, it had to ask the land where best its urgent passage would be accepted. The curves it could form were limited by the rigidity of rails; the grades it could master were governed by the human capacity to move the tons of steel that would pass along them.

Yes, there were tunnels blasted and mountains sheared, and in that we can take no great pride. But, when all the efforts of dynamite and shovel were done, this was still an effort measured on human scale, a rough relative to the breaking of branches and the slashing of trees.

Men with hammers and shovels were not so far removed from men with adzes made of sharpened stone. And dynamite, though possessed of compressed power and the force of sudden impact, was still, at heart, little more than a magnifier and an ally in the task of moving stone and debris so that the great mechanized pack animal of the railroad could find a narrow path that would accept its passage.

But more than that, the routes it chose bore the echoes of the Native people who had wandered the land for aeons and had followed the hunting trails of animals until they knew it with the intimacy of skin.

Not so, the freeway. These are passages seen from Shiva's eye.

Who among us has not been surprised at how different the land feels when we descend from the freeways to the streets of a town? We attribute this to the speed of our travel, to the fact that our trip is buffered from the intimate

Kent Nerburn

punctuations of stop-and-go.

But he real reason lies deeper, with the indifference of the freeway to the land. Even those men who, centuries ago, dropped that heartless surveyor's grid across the midsection of our continent were unable to defeat the stronger forces of the land.

Economic necessity and the limitations of technology dictated that even their roads must meet defeat in the face of river bottoms and great marshy expanses.

With a shy curtsy to necessity, they moved to the left or right, or bent their gridlines to acknowledge the great indifference of the earthen forms that they could neither seduce nor tame.

But the freeways make no such apologies. They ride like bridges on the land — parapets of concrete that carry us like potentates upon their shoulders, buffered from the bumps and idiosyncrasies of the earth over which we pass.

With the tools of modern land moving technology we have democratized the experience of passage into standardized gradients and ruler-edged straightaways. We have taken the natural rhythms of the land and made them into the normative rhythms of the engineer's drawing board.

This is not so vast a loss as that which comes from lifting off the earth and landing again, hopping from island of civilization to island of civilization with no meaningful sense of passage. But it is a loss nonetheless, for it takes us one step further from the aesthetics of the land.

And it is in the aesthetics — the rhythm, the texture, the color, the timbre — that we find justification for listening to her voice. We will save that which we love, and we love best that which we have felt and understood in all its beauty.

We cannot go back, at least not without cataclysm. Perhaps that is coming on its own. But, in lieu of it, we must travel back, back in our minds and hearts, from the highways to the roadways to the pathways and the trails. We must see something original and indigenous in that which is modern.

Then, perhaps, we can glimpse, if only as a dream, the land that was once known as a mother.

Then, perhaps, the ancient pathways will beckon to us once again.

Kent Nerburn

Kent Nerburn

⟨ SEEKING HOME ⟩

I rise, I rise,
I, in whose humped shoulder there is power.

— Osage rite of vigil for the
rising of the buffalo men

The hills rise and fall, rise and fall, becoming a rhythm and a motion. I am on a motorcycle, traveling across Montana, on the last thin line of roadway that hugs our northern border.

It is August and the sun is behind me. It burns on my neck, pushing me forward — against the westward flow of history, back toward the east, back toward my home.

Heat, motion, return — broad knowledges, greater than the self.

I must savor this, I tell myself. Forget thought, forget destination, find a grace in rhythm and motion, like a dancer transcending craft and pattern to become a pure experience of joy.

But the heat will not relent. The sun is an angry bead, forgiving nothing. The roadway shimmers; the brown hills droop. Colors on the hillside touch some corner of my childhood and I am off, floating free, awash in allusion, where memory touches dream.

As I come over a rise I see a structure far ahead of me. It is small, three-sided, like a life-sized crèche, or an enclosure for a spring. It sits in lonely isolation — singular, like a cairn, in the center of a great bowl of land.

Abruptly, I am brought back. The structure rivets me, anchors my attention, like a sharp sound in the night. Nothing else intrudes on the landscape; no other work of human hand breaks the motion of the land.

I ease in before it. The heat swoops in upon me like a bird of prey. The wind, arid and relentless, burns my face. The air sears my lungs.

I walk, crunching, across the roadway. Heat rises from the pavement. Sweat soaks the neck of my shirt. The enclosure beckons me with shade, protection, sanctuary.

Through its open front I can see a small pen made of posts and planking. Inside there is a large object. As my eyes adjust, I see that it is a rock, a boulder even, in the rough form of a large animal — buffalo or ox — lying as if at rest.

There is a plaque nearby, telling me that this is a buffalo rock of the kind held sacred by the Lakota, or Sioux. It was found on a nearby hillside and transported to this spot as part of some historical marker program.

The tone of the plaque is respectful. It speaks of the Sioux legacy and never refers to Native belief as myth. It is full of information about the rock — age, material, and places where one can find the tool marks of the unknown craftsman who tried to coax a finished image from the stone.

I try to look more closely at the rock, but I cannot. The fence obscures my view. I could climb over; it is only slats, and only two feet high.

Instead, I step back. I am a creature of my culture. To reach across a barrier, a boundary, is to violate. To lean over a fence is to betray a border. I move to the respectful distance commanded not by the rock, but by the fence.

Somewhere, centuries ago and miles away, a man walking on this ancient seabed came upon this boulder. In its rude form he saw the inchoate shape of the buffalo. With ritual observances now lost to our hearts, he took another harder stone and began chipping away, trying to release or clarify the form.

Kent Nerburn

Did he sing to the buffalo as he worked?

Did he feel the spirit of the great beast guiding his hand?

Was he seeking to claim spiritual power by creating a simulacrum; to assert a spiritual affinity that would give him power over this greatest of animals that gave food, shelter, clothing, and the very sustenance of life to his people?

Was he, like me, seared by this blazing heat and stung by the sand and silt carried on this heartless wind?

Or did he labor with frozen hands in frigid winter snows?

Perhaps he waited for those few kind hours and days and months when such labor was congenial, and worked only then, as year followed upon year, until he had devoted his entire life to the shaping of this stone.

Or perhaps he worked only under certain moons, or when he heard the buffalo calling in the night.

A deep sadness overwhelms me. There is a wrongness here.

Why is this rock enclosed in a pen like an animal? Did someone fear its escape? Must its wildness be penned, its roughness set apart, lest it sink back into the landscape and become but one more stone upon the earth?

The poignancy of the metaphor floods across me: the living belief of this land's first people reduced to a placard and made into a roadside attraction to feed the intellectual curiosity of the American public; the power of the earth, named, framed, and incarcerated inside a fence.

Behind me, the wind moves across the land like the devil's breath. Before me, the rock huddles in its pen in forlorn isolation. I stand between, under walls and roof, protected from nature, full of information, separated from faith.

The base of the pen has been filled with gravel to the depth of about a foot. The rock sits upon the gravel which sits upon a concrete slab. What was once a hallowing has become a presentation. What was once sacred has been reduced to mere importance. And all of it — the enclosure, the fencing, the lifting off the earth — bears silent witness to the fact of separation.

The rock is massive, the size of a young buffalo calf. The thought of transporting it to this spot it conjures up images of fork lifts, flatbeds, and wheezing hydraulics. Men without modern equipment, intent upon its movement, might, with levers and fulcrums, in the course of a day have rolled it a quarter of a mile, and then only on level ground.

But such movement was unlikely. The craftsman who set his hand to this boulder would never have considered such an act. To him, this rock was part of the land, as surely as a tree or river, never to be moved. By working it, he, in some fashion, consecrated the ground where it lay. He would be aghast, even filled with terror, if he were to see it now, placed and penned beside a roadway in a wooden shed.

What act, I think, would he perform? What prayer would he offer to restore the natural order?

I move in closer.

In a hollow on the back of the boulder I see two cigarettes. They have been broken at the middle, allowing the tobacco to spill out upon the stone. It is an act of consecration common to the Indian people.

In a gesture as humble as a Catholic's genuflection before the Blessed Sacrament, some unknown person has honored the spirit of the great beast that embodies all the bounty of the earth to the Sioux people. But, more than that, this passerby, as anonymous as the craftsman who shaped the boulder, has paid homage to Wakan Tanka, the Creator, whose immutability and

Kent Nerburn

eternal steadfastness are seen as incarnated in the character of every stone.

I reach over the fence and place my hands on the rock.

Its coolness is deep, deeper than the parching of the sun.

My fingers find the chip marks, and I touch the labor of another across the barrier of time.

I move my hands along the hump, down the back. I am overcome by the solidity, the permanence. Idea has become presence, and I want to lie down against the rock and sleep.

It is late. The sun outside has turned the hills to ochre, the color of the stone. Shadows have begun to creep along the draws. The hot winds that penetrate the walls rustle the tobacco, causing it to move as if it were alive.

I leave the enclosure and walk back across the searing pavement to my motorcycle. The asphalt, like the concrete slab and the bed of gravel, separates me and defines my understanding. It is a causeway, a mapping, a shaping of cognition and experience.

The rock has receded into shadow.

I set my course down the ribbon of roadway and head off toward the east, like a man fleeing from the sunset.

Kent Nerburn

TRAILER WOMAN

My fathers,
My mothers,
In some little hollow,
In some low brush,
You will reveal yourselves to me.

—Zuni stalking prayer

She stands, sallow and hollow-eyed, beside the trailer in a faded print dress, hanging out laundry. Her eyes mark my passing, but do not follow.

I have seen this trailer many times before. It sits forlornly, defiantly, on a patch of barren ground beside the road in this unpeopled landscape of bog and bramble. The earth around it has been worn to dirt, then overgrown with weeds, then worn again to dirt by the passages of families who come, stay a month or a winter, then move on without notice or remorse, leaving behind piles of garbage and the rotted carcasses of old cars.

The trailer is a beacon, a marker on this odd forty-nine-mile stretch of forgotten road.

Twenty eight miles south lies a dying main street farm town, the last outpost of the rich, deciduous forests and farmlands of the Midwest; twenty one miles north sits a convenience store and gas station, marking the entrance into the deep green of the northern boreal forests. Between, there is only this expanse of stunted tamarack and bracken, and the road exists only to permit safe passage.

I know this road well. It was created to secure the support of some long dead local congressman who had sold his vote to the city folks in exchange for a roadway that few would use and none would need.

It was built, marked, and forgotten.

Winter freezes and the marshy landscape have buckled it until in some places it is now a tracery of fissures and asphalt scabs. Truckers use it, as do locals and travelers who are not afraid of its dreary isolation.

You drive it to survive it. It is the road to my home.

I am traveling quickly. But still, as I pass the trailer, I can see a change. Three children's bicycles are lined against the skirting near the steps. There are lace curtains in the window. Clothes hang clean and bleached on a single line.

A rusted green Ford sits with its right front brake drum resting on a cement block. It has been like this for months, since long before the woman and her family moved in. The hood is open, as it has been each time I have passed this way.

"It must be sprung," I tell myself, "or she would surely have shut it." Open car hoods, like open cupboard doors, speak of incompletion and inattention.

This woman has raked the dirt surrounding the trailer. She would not leave a car hood unhinged, like a broken jaw, unless it were beyond her to force it closed.

"But what of her husband?" I think.

I know he exists. His faded flannel shirts hang splayed on the line, like scarecrows who have fled. Surely he can push that sprung tongue of metal back in place.

I try to imagine him. A pickup truck sits beside the trailer. It is old, huge, dirty. The bed is filled with oily engine blocks and axles.

This is country where men's lives center around vehicles. There is

Kent Nerburn

no work, so mobility is the only commodity of value. Manhood, hope, and freedom are tied to them. To own them, to fix them, to drive them, to trade them, is the only victory available in this joyless place. A man who lives here can shut a car hood, any car hood

A shaft of dancing light reflects from a pile of brown beer bottles lying in a fire pit on the margin of the dirt clearing.

He drinks beer. He drinks it from bottles. He drinks it at home.

I am past now. The bog and brush close in around the road. The undergrowth claws at the pavement, eyes of low animals peer from the roadside underbrush. Gravel side roads turn off to nowhere. From November to March they will be filled with trackless snow.

The woman's face will not leave me. Parchment over bones, with sadness etched in every line.

I try to grant her the possibility of hope. But it will not work. I have watched this trailer for seven years, and it will allow me no delusions.

How to explain this? Other houses, empty as skulls, stand abandoned along this lonely, barren road. Other trailers, as torn and beaten as this, dot the sparse fields in similar mute isolation. But they all, in some measure, speak of hope that has fled. Collapsing barns, rusting combines—something once proud, now abandoned, marks their passage into desolation.

Not so, this trailer. It stands in naked and angry defiance against any impulse toward human decency. There is no garage to hint of projects or protection. No driveway has ever been carved or marked. The few small tamaracks that have had made their way up through the earth near the house have been snapped off and left like exposed femurs sticking from the ground. There is no promise of redemption anywhere.

It is an outlaw's house, this trailer — a man's house, a drunk's house, with no sense of amenity or domestic grace. It is too far from any town to be a base for a richer and more promising life. The land around is too marshy to grow crops; the fields are too barren to support livestock.

The whole setting speaks of brutality and despair. And seven years of comings and goings of tenants have not changed its presence. This is a place for misfits, for runners, for brutish men with seedy eyes to drink beer, molest their daughters, and fall asleep in front of televisions.

I have always loathed this trailer. It has none of that sense of mystery that lonely homesteads fire in the imagination.

Many times, I would pass it late at night and it would fill me with dread. The lights, when there were any, were always stark. It never drew me for a moment to imagine myself inside it, sitting cozy at the kitchen table during winter storms. I feared the lives that were lived within.

Slowly, I have begun to see it as a curse. I have passed it now many dozens of times. And each time I have searched for signs of hope, of promise, of growth. But there have been none.

One family would come, leave, and be replaced by another.

One time it would be a broken Chevy jacked up in the yard, the next time an Oldsmobile. A pile of broken motorcycles would appear near the door, then be gone, their place taken by bags of garbage thrown haphazardly from the steps. One or three or seven dirty children would be grubbing in the dirt. Then it would be abandoned, dark, with hanging screens and no front door.

One time, in the deepest winter we had known for decades, someone had put a plastic Christmas candle in a window. It glowed red and proud against the darkness. The next month, it was gone, along with the footprints and the people and the ruts of the cars in the snow. In their place was a trackless plain of windswept white with drifts blown two feet high against the door. A shred of cloth blew and flapped through an empty, broken window.

Kent Nerburn

It was not until the following spring that the trailer came alive again. This time there was an evil transience about it. Three and four cars at a time would be parked outside. Usually one of them had its hood open, though I never saw anyone working on the engines. Beer cans littered the yard like stones.

Then, this, too, was gone. Only the green Ford, with its sprung hood, remained. Bags of garbage were piled ceiling high in its back seat.

And now there is the woman and her lace curtains. I want to turn around and go back to her. I want to talk to her. But I don't. Her husband, toothless and full of beer, sits somewhere nearby. Though there may be no love between them, suspicion is the last emotion to die. A stranger stopping in the yard for no reason other than to talk has the spore of an intruder.

I drive another mile. The sun, to my left, is a ball of fire over the marshland. It is yet a hundred miles to my home.

I turn into one of the gravel roads, reverse the car, and turn around.

My heart is pounding. I drive back toward the south. The break in the scrub and brush looms ahead. I reach into the glove box and pull out a map and shake it wildly until it falls open on the floor.

The woman is still standing by the line. She has a clothespin in her mouth. She looks up as I turn in. A curtain moves in the trailer.

I get out.

She turns to face me and takes a step toward the house. Her bony arms are crossed against her chest as if against an attacker.

"Excuse me," I say. "Could you tell me where the road to Nevis is?" I hold up the map as proof of my good intentions.

"Back there," she points. She keeps her elbows to her side and covers her mouth with her hand, as if she has revealed too much.

"Thanks," I say. "Not much on this road."

She shakes her head quickly in frightened agreement. The shirts and underwear on the line are a gleaming white.

Again the curtain moves.

I turn and walk toward the truck. The sun glints amber against the pile of beer bottles.

"What's wrong with the car?" I ask, pointing to the abandoned Ford.

"It's not ours," she responds.

In a far corner, hidden from the road by a line of tamaracks, I see a small garden. Clumpy vegetables protrude like dolls' heads from the ground. Seed packs are stuck on sticks at the beginning of each row.

"Thanks," I say, and get back in my car. The woman goes quickly into the house.

It is six weeks before I pass again. The blaze of fall has come and gone. The wind is colder now than the air. The swamp grasses are grey and withered.

I glance at the trailer as I pass. It is empty. The line where the clothes had hung is gone.

I pull over cautiously. Nothing moves. The screenless storm door squeaks idly in the wind. There are no curtains.

I look to the garden. It is kicked, stomped, willfully mangled and destroyed. The seed packets lie half buried in the dirt.

The green Ford sits, untouched, unmoved. The bags of garbage are still in its back seat. I reach up and grab the hood. It moves easily.

I hesitate for a second, then bring it down and hook it to its latch, trying hard not to make a sound.

Kent Nerburn

The hint of winter on a distant wind.

The haunted still before a storm.

Silence is the vesper of the land, as powerful as

shadow, as haunting as the moon.

Solitudes

"The holy silence is God's voice."

— Ohiyesa
Santee Sioux

Kent Nerburn

WINTERWATCH

"May I see the spring. May I with all my people safely reach it."
— Crow prayer

We know it is coming. We can see it in the animals' eyes.

The sky is too cold; the wind, too raw. Leaden clouds loom heavy on the horizon. Darkness grows stronger than light. The affairs of day begin and end now in shadow.

I turn my eyes to the northwest. There is a sound there, beneath hearing, like the distant rhythm of an approaching army. In its cadence is the heavy breath of winter.

I watch uneasily, full of dark presentiments of blizzards, remembering the times when I lost the road and the wind would not subside, and the great unfeeling cold moved indifferently against me, beginning at the toes and fingers and coaxing me to the drowsiness I have been taught so long to fear.

In these dark memories the terror still resides, of another winter stretching insurmountable in time and circumstance. And all of us in this northern place dream of fleeing to the warmlands where the colors do not fade.

But we do not. We stay.

Still, our fears grow greater than our faith. Will this be the winter we do not live to see the spring?

It was last year, I think, when the man who brings the heating oil told me of the old couple, in their nineties, who sat together, alone, in the farm they would not leave, without heat, huddled together under a blanket, until some passerby found them in their starvation and incontinence, and the woman was taken to a nursing home and the man to a neighbor's house where he wanders, wide-eyed and deranged, calling out names no one has ever heard.

And the memory, told by the Ojibwe north of me, of the man who came from Wyoming to make his fortune, and had horses shipped by rail to graze on the cheap farmland where no hand had been able to coax a crop to grow.

And left them, as he took to shelter miles away to weather out the winter storms, convinced that they would find their forage easily beneath the snow, until the passing neighbors found them starved and frozen, like boulders of skeleton and hide, half covered by the drifting snows, their flanks pressed hard against a stand of oaks.

The man went back to Wyoming, so the story goes, but the old men still remember, and the children still play their summer games beneath the trees where the horses huddled, froze, and died; and call the land "starvation grove," as if so hideous a name comes naturally and marks the land as easily as "muddy creek" or "turtle hill."

And always, it is the same. Everything was fine "until." And then the passing neighbor or deliveryman, alerted by the absence of tracks, discovers.
. .

Until. Until. There is the measurement of our fear. Will we be able to last "until?" Will there be enough to carry us "until?" Are we strong enough, in body and in spirit, to endure "until?"

It is the "until" we fear, that the desperate cry to get to us in time will be swallowed up into the trackless silence that neither judges nor forgives.

We are sailors here, upon this inland winter sea, and brothers and sisters to the children of the desert. We share the common knowledge that

Kent Nerburn

our lives can disappear without a trace. We need not move; we need not seek. We need not court some precipice of danger. We need only be heedless of the voice of nature, and that which splits our consciousness from hers will be gone, absorbed into the oneness that we so desire and so fear.

Yes, these are lands that make us holy. Not some bacchanal of spirit light burst full flower from within, but the holy fear wrought by thundergods — demanding, indifferent, needing supplication lest they should look closely down upon us as they pass.

A sound flutters above me. A flock of geese, grey and urgent, comes out of the sky from the northwest, passes honking overhead, and disappears. Their mystical precision seems more driven today.

A flake, solitary messenger, winds its way among the leafless trees and settles on the earth.

There is distance in the air.

BENEDICTION

Drifting snow,
Why do I sing?

— Ojibwe song

The snow came again last night. She left before the dawn, bestowing in her wake a benediction upon the earth. Now, in morning light, she greets us gently, a prayer shawl donned upon the land.

Here and there a whirling gust, whipped up by some angry and isolated wind, rises tiny and intense like a petulant child trying to start a fight.

But this is not his day. The world is silent and at peace, and the tracks and markings we have made upon the earth, the endless measurements and passages, are again forgiven.

I hold my breath. All is white and still. The pines stand in steepled reverence against the sky. The elms reach out their fingers in naked supplication. And the birch, kindred spirits to the winter earth, show off their white and graceful elegance against the mantle of their sister, snow. Far in the distance, the thin line of forest is a lacework tracery, flashing diamonds of crystal light against the cold brilliance of the day.

A fox braves the brightness of the morning sun and rushes across the fresh eternity, for a moment immortal, like the first shooting star that ever cut across an evening sky.

He bounds and scrabbles, crazed by his blind exposure, then disappears into the distant woods. But he is not followed. This is not a time of hunting. The world still wakes in gentle wonder; it is not yet a time of passions and of fears.

It makes the heart gentle, this snow, burying the sharp edges of life and cutting us off from time. Our traces on the surface of the land are gone; our lives devoid of history once more. All is singular; all is one. We are children at the dawn of time.

Begin again. Begin again. This snowfall says, begin again. It is the purest absolution, and falls in vast forgiveness on us all.

Kent Nerburn

BLUE

I smoke with the Great Spirit.
Let us have a blue day.

—Sioux song

I walked today, knee deep in snow that had a sparkle on its surface. Each footstep lifted clouds of winter diamonds, azure blue and crystalline, like firesparks of ice.

It is a day of blue, this winter morning. The blue-hued snow betrays its water source within. Tree trunks echo blue in sympathetic harmony.

Even the wind blows blue — cool, edgy, soothing and serene. And above it all a cobalt sky vaults insurmountable in cloudless brilliance, casting shadows long and lavender across the land.

It is the palette of a genius painter, this winter day; a Chinese watercolor, but with edges sharp and cutting as a knife.

If you would live in winter, you must give yourself to blue. Not as a color, or as a wistful sadness, but as a distance, receding from the surface, that turns at every point to meditation. It is like the echo in a vast architecture, a footfall in a great cathedral.

I step. The snow crusts beneath me. Its surface breaks like the shattering of glass. Above me, a jay perches, then swoops, his actions leaving no track or trace, his flight a fugue against the sky.

Not so, with me. The tracks I leave do not return to stillness, but shape a landscape of intent. Into the blue soliloquy I send a march, a cadence with a purpose.

On days like this I do not love our mortal grounding. I am revealed too much for who I am. I can push forward into endless purity. But if I turn, as honesty demands, I see my history revealed, and my single path betrays the gentle vesper of the land.

We may, as Wordsworth says, come trailing clouds of glory. But once that glory touches down, we leave our mark.

I would rather seek the margins of the woods than cut a razor path across the land.

If I must live in counterpoint, let it be a gentle sound.

Kent Nerburn

The land now is darkening. All human connection is lost.
Each house is solitary, full of its own despair or love.
No sun sets; evening is but a fading of the day.
And the wind howls lonely in the growing, purpling dark.

Darkenings

Toward me the great darkness comes rattling

— Papago song

Kent Nerburn

JANUARY

The strong night is shaking me

— Pima song

The dark is too long now.

It is only eight, and already I dream of sleep. I pace, unnerved and unbalanced, anger seeking a place to land.

The Sioux have named it well, this month — January: The Moon of Great Difficulty.

December is still human, its holiday anticipation dominating over the darkening winter. February breaks and shatters, each day alive with new possibility.

But January is solid and unrelenting. The sky does not change. The clouds do not move. Only direction is real, and the only real direction is north. We await change as if it were a messenger.

All the small movements now echo large. A rabbit running across the snow. The scrape of a spoon against a bowl. A change in light.

Nighttime winds shake the house like an angry father throttling an infant. All senses are alert. Every nuance thunders. This is the time when the Ojibwe told their tales. A child who heard a story in deep winter carried it forever in his heart.

This is also the time when madmen run naked across the snows and husbands kill their wives in bed. A strange sound becomes more real than a common one. A hopeless dream can send a person into frenzy.

You must look closely in this dark month. Examine the backs of your hands and the movements of your fingers. Place your thumbprints on

the edges of old bowls. Immerse yourself in ceremonies of the ordinary.
Do not seek large issues. In January one needs ritual, not philosophy.

Kent Nerburn

— ‹ NATIVITY ›—

What is life?
. . . It is the breath of the buffalo in the winter time.
—Blackfeet death oration

He fixes his gaze upon me. His breath is strong; his nostrils create wind.

Clearly he has culled me out. Even the rancher has noticed, and gently admonishes me to move around the front of the truck. There is no urgency in his voice, but his directions are pointed.

"He's a new one," he says, sounding almost apologetic. "I just got him from Custer State Park. Don't know him too well yet."

Then, almost as an afterthought, he adds, "They are wild animals, you know. You can never totally trust them."

The buffalo stares at me with dark, flat eyes. He must stand six feet or more at the shoulder. My eyes are even with his hump.

"They're not aggressive animals," he continues. "Very territorial, though. They'll do what they have to to move you out of their space."

I look at the horns. Ohiyesa, the Santee Sioux writer, once observed that if attacked by a grizzly, you should pick up a sharp stick and thrust it toward him, for all animals, save a starving grey wolf, fear the power of horns.

The bull stares darkly.

The thin wall of the pickup is a fool's delusion, and I know it. He knows it too. He knows many things. His curiosity has not been without purpose as he has been watching me. He has been gaining knowledge, but it is knowledge of the senses. He has been measuring my fear.

I think back to Ohiyesa's story of the great Lakota warrior, Tomahay. He had hopped on a buffalo's back and ridden him to the earth.

Face to face with the malevolent indifference of this bull, such courage seems unbelievable.

"They stand into the wind," the rancher is saying. "When they are threatened they form a circle, face out, with the calves at the center. Just like the wagon trains."

"Or an Indian camp," I observe.

"Always watch the animals," the elders had counseled. "They will tell you how to live."

The Ojibwe chose their leaders from the Crane clan, because the crane spoke only seldom, and when it did, all other animals listened.

The Dakota hunters taught their children to follow the practice of the wolf, and always take one final look, even in retreat, to gain further knowledge.

"What else does the buffalo do?" I ask.

"They can escape from anything," the rancher responds.

He enjoys telling of his herd. "I can build a fence ten feet high, and they'll climb over it like a dog if they want to. But if they like their land, they'll stay there with less fence than a pig would need. Sometimes they'll break down a fence to get in to their land. Their land is very important to them."

The Dakota in southwestern Minnesota, forced into an exile of poverty and squalor in the prairies of South Dakota, had walked the hundreds of miles back to their native land and repurchased it with handfuls of pennies and dollars.

Kent Nerburn

The rancher is still talking. "They form groups, like extended families. They will protect each other. They take care of all the young, even if they aren't their own. It's really something to see."

The bull has wandered off. I breathe more easily.

We drive deeper into the valley. The buffalo follow us, surrounding us each time we stop to give them feed. I get out one more time to help. They number in the dozens, close maybe to a hundred. By their mere scale and number they make me wary.

In the wild, face to face, there comes a moment when there is a measuring between species. Each is aware of its power, each is aware of its vulnerability. You lock into each other's presence, and in an instant you know. It is an issue of dominance. All is decided, all is resolved. You bow your heads to the knowledge. Survival demands it.

He is there again.

I could not have recognized him by appearances, could not have chosen him from among the others by sight. But his stillness is different. He is specific in his purpose, focused in his gaze. He is looking at me.

"That's the Custer bull," I say to the rancher, a false brightness in my voice. If the rancher knows my fear, he does not let on. He has brought me here, and does not want to acknowledge an error.

"Yes," he says, and goes back to pouring the feed into piles on the frozen ground.

I inch back to the truck door and climb in, full of a private shame.

The animals move in closer, tossing their heads from side to side to clear their eating space with their horns. They surround the truck, pushing to within a foot of it on all sides. Their heads are larger than the window. The

Custer bull remains apart.

My fear grows again. We are far into the valley. The truck is a clumsy animal that can only move on cleared paths. Its armor is thin; it turns gracelessly and slowly. The bull is distant and impassive. If he is not going to feed, why has he followed?

"Do they ever charge?" I yell to the rancher. He is busy placing the feed sack back in the pickup bed.

"They're wild animals," he says again. "They're unpredictable. I don't turn my back on them."

The buffalo are on all sides of the truck, brushing against it. I can see the Custer bull on the hill, watching.

I begin to impute motives to him. What have I done to offend him? What can he sense about me? Do I contain an arrogance?

His indifference seems like hate; his preoccupation, a measuring. He has become a judgment, a damnation. Creation is ruling against me.

I reach down to pet the dog who has ridden along. His ranch life is full of freedom, but lacks the warmth of human contact. He has taken to me instantly for my willing banter and playful cuffing. His friendliness is a comfort.

He nuzzles against me. His rough fur seems to offer me protection.

"See," I want to say to the bull, "the dog likes me."

The bull stands silently against the hillside. He is darker now against the woods and trees. Night has begun to descend, and the wind is raising sheets of blowing snow.

There is an Ojibwe tale about a meeting of the animals. They had gathered to discuss how to deal with Man, who was killing too many of them. It was decided that the animals should kill Man. The dog, hearing this, had run off to inform Man.

A vigilant wolf spied the escaping dog and followed him on his mission, then dragged him back to the assembly of the animals. It was decided that for his punishment, the dog should be forever bound to Man and dependent upon him.

He was to live his life a supplicant to the human, banished for all time from the brotherhood of the wild ones.

The dog whimpers and pants and presses against me. His eagerness seems servile.

"Best get back before dark," the rancher is saying. He has finished the feeding.

He pulls the pickup door open a crack and slides in. The buffalo jump back at the movement of the door. Their grace astounds me.

He shoves the pickup into gear and moves forward slowly. The animals part as he noses among them. Their heads, large as oil drums, turn toward us and they stare at us with blank, liquid eyes. There is barely enough room for us to pass.

The sky has given up all vestiges of daylight. The valley is bathed in purple dark. The buffalo stand among the trees and on the hillside and in circles around the piles of feed. They are no more than shadows.

The Custer bull has not moved. He turns his head slightly to mark our passage. How has he found a spot so distant as to show disdain, so close as to imply threat?

The rancher begins speaking with animation about his decision to switch to buffalo from cattle.

"They really are a perfect food," he says. "Low cholesterol. Full of protein. People don't realize it. Great ranching opportunity. There are so few of them out there — maybe a couple hundred thousand — that the big corporations can't muscle in. It isn't worth their time."

In the mid-1800's, it was reported, the numbers of the buffalo were so great that travelers had to wait three days for a single herd to pass. Hunting expeditions were organized for wealthy eastern tourists to travel west and shoot buffalo from the train. They did not even have to put their feet on the ground. Photographs abound of settlers standing on piles of buffalo skulls, as wide as houses, as tall as trees.

"One more stop," the rancher says. "Got to feed the blind one." He pulls up to a penned area. A mother and young calf are standing near the fence.

"Come on," he says.

I looked around for the bull; he is nowhere to be seen.

I get out of the pickup. The rancher is already pouring feed from a white burlap bag.

The mother stands before me, staring blankly. Her head is a boulder; her hump a tiny mountain. In a storm, or a battle, one could hide behind her carcass and survive.

She stares with idle curiosity. The young calf nuzzles against her flank. He, too, knows the power of her protection.

I look at his eyes. They are grey and milky, as large as my fist.

The mother turns her head toward me. For an instant there is recognition.

"Time to get back," the rancher observes.

Shapes move on the hillside. We make our way toward the house, stopping only to latch the gate to the valley.

Kent Nerburn

Once inside his house, the rancher shows me his trophies: a mounted buffalo head on the wall above the piano where his daughter is working her way haltingly through a Mozart minuet; a stuffed baby buffalo calf sitting stiff-legged on a rug in the hallway.

"Died after just a few days. Lots of people who come in here think she's real." We stand by the freezer, talking, as the night increases outside.

I mention the white buffalo.

Many winters ago, it is said, two Lakota warriors saw a beautiful woman on a hillside. The one approached her with bad intentions and was reduced to ash and bones. The other respected her, and brought her to the village where she gave the people the sacred pipe by which they would forever be connected to the Great Mystery. She then told them she would return to them some day.

As she walked away, she turned into a white buffalo.

Now, it has been reported, a white buffalo calf has been born on a farm in Wisconsin. People, Native and non-Native alike, have been thronging to see it. Offers to buy it have come from as far away as the Middle East.

"It's changing color," the rancher laughs. "The guy should have sold it while he had a chance."

The rancher keeps me a bit longer, telling me about the nutritional aspects of buffalo and the great future they have in the marketplace. By the time I leave the sky is alive with purple night. Stars are bursting forth in handfuls in the clear winter air.

I walk down the hill toward my truck, then stop. Sounds of heavy movement are coming from the draw.

I make my way through the crunching snow to where the dark forms stand outlined in the winter dark. The mother and her blind calf are still standing in the pen. She turns her head toward me and grunts.

I inch closer to the calf. Vaporous streams rise like spirits from his nostrils. There is a moistness in his eyes, upon his nose. All about him is a rank sweetness, a commingling of innocence and lust, a potency as powerful as murder, as guileless as the dawn.

I reach to touch him, but draw back. The grey emptiness of his sightless eyes glows silver in the narrow moonlight. He drops his head against his mother. In the darkness they become as one.

Further up the valley I can feel the sudden undertow of movement. Shapes are shifting, turning. Shadows emerge from among the far off trees. The woods are marching.

I step back and start to retreat. The shadows move patiently, relentlessly, without anger or fear. Steam rises from them into the winter air. I want to run, but do not. The mother has closed in around her calf. His eyes are blank as river stones.

I reach into my pocket and grab some feed. I lay it before the calf, like frankincense or myrrh, and hurry toward the draw. The earth cracks beneath my feet in violation of the silence. I dare not run.

I turn to look, one last time. The shadows have formed a circle surrounding the pen. They stand, motionless, each head pointing outward. The blind calf is bent over, oblivious, feeding on the grain left by my hand.

In the distant forest shapes still move among the trees. On the hill by the house the dog barks, and the halting strains of Mozart drift muffled through the frigid winter night. Far above me the Pleiades twinkle with an icy brightness. The sky has exploded with stars.

From deep in the draw I feel the singular presence of intention. The valley sings out with the almost unbearable presence of life.

Kent Nerburn

Kent Nerburn

WINTER MAN

The wolf on the open prairie and the silver-tip bear, a near cousin to the grizzly, will sometimes take a fancy to keep company with you for several miles, if he thinks you do not see him.

—Ohiyesa
Santee Sioux

He stands in the swirling snow by the side of the road, hidden by the wind. He is not hitchhiking; he makes no gesture toward the passing cars.

It is his stillness that transfixes me.

He is a sentinel in the storm, a dark object unresponsive to the torrents of movement raging around him. Only by intention could one remain so still. The silence of his power makes me feel afraid.

The wind beats at the window and batters the car in shuddering gusts. The snow leaps and swirls, clawing like a desperate animal, trying angrily to force itself through cracks, its icy breath seeking places to attack.

The heater blows a fragile warmth. The windshield wipers cut a sweeping arc that fades and disappears. I turn the radio up loud.

But still, he stands.

I pull slowly to a stop before him. He walks toward me as if he has been waiting. He slides silently into the seat beside me, shutting the door against the angry violence of the wind.

"Going to the reservation?" I ask.

He nods without turning.

"Cold out there," I venture.

He says nothing, stares straight ahead.

I have seen him before. His long, grey hair and craggy face are singular, untouched by generations. Once you have seen him he takes root in your memory.

He sits unmoving in the seat beside me. His eyes are avian, seeing far and minute, looking for a single movement or a hint of meaning in the violent storm that rages around us.

It is an attitude of vigilance, one that I have only seen in animals. He is like a cat waiting to pounce, or a wolf following the movements of his prey — a coiled fury that the casual observer might even mistake for sleep.

I try again to engage him. "Rough day to be out."

His silence mocks my words, reducing them to noise. To speak to him is to be the loud and clumsy child destroying the silence of the forest.

I turn off the radio. The sound of the storm swoops in.

I grip tighter on the wheel. The snow is falling in sheets. The stands of trees are becoming indistinct grey masses. Snow dust rips by in front of me, obscuring the road.

"Going to lose the road soon," I say, hoping he will tell me to turn back. But he says nothing.

The wind unleashes a graveyard howl and buffets the car.

Fear rises in my throat. There are still twenty miles to the reservation, and the road is drifting over with snow.

The old man takes out a cigarette and strikes a match, neither offering nor asking. Droplets of water drip from his long, grey hair. He sits back and smokes as I grip the wheel with both hands. He does not look at me. I hear him breathing and smell the odor of the tobacco and his breath.

I cannot fathom his stillness. He is like a man going off to die. He draws patiently, silently, on the cigarette, and stares straight ahead.

Suddenly he gestures and makes a sound. His voice is low, barely a

Kent Nerburn

rasp.

I look where he is pointing. I can see nothing.

He wheezes a brittle rattle and crushes his cigarette between his thumb and forefinger. From the side of my eyes I can see that his lips are curled in a tiny smile.

I do not want to be in the car with this man. I do not want to drive further. The sky through the snow is a ghostly pewter.

He rasps again, the sound of dry leaves or an animal moving through cattails.

"Stop," he says.

A spike of panic runs through me. We are miles from houses. In the swirling storm the forest has no shape.

I look wildly toward him, afraid he has a gun.

He gestures with a clawed hand toward the side of the road. "Right here."

I stop the car. The crunching of my tires in the trackless snow makes a final sound, then falls silent. The wind wails. The woods close in. I can feel my heart pounding in my chest.

He pushes the door open against the wind. Snow swirls in and covers the seat. Without thanks or explanation he steps from the car and walks toward the woods. There are no roads, no houses, not even a trail.

I want to shout after him, to offer him a jacket. But the storm has closed around him.

For a second, amid my fear and confusion, I feel more alone than I have in my entire life.

URN

How I go shivering. . .
Where is the sun hiding his fire?

— Iroquois ritual chant

We have not seen zero for days. Daylight is a brief spasm between darknesses. The sun is wrong and evil; like a father without love, grinning.

All the news now is of deaths. On icy roads, in frozen houses, in fires that flashed from desperate hands trying to stoke a stove to warmth.

The old are helpless, trapped. The deer are starving. There are no birds anywhere.

Midnight. I step outside. There is a crazed brightness in the sky, like the gaze of one about to die. The moon is remorseless — an adder's eye, watching for movement, looking for death.

Trees explode, their frozen sap no longer able to endure. The lake rends and thunders beneath the frozen snows. Dogs rise from their burrows and howl in frenzy at the sounds. Their voices break the night like glass.

Forty below. Morning light, and pale. I stop at a small store beside the highway. It is a country place, part gas station, part commissary, sparsely stocked. Old men sit on cases of Coke and boxes of motor oil, telling stories of the cold.

"I need to make a call," I say.

They gesture. A back room, tires and cardboard boxes, a pay phone hanging on the wall. A man is on the phone — thirties, ashen, missing teeth. His girlfriend smiles weakly at me. She is hunched in a corner. Their jackets are thin.

"Long or short," I ask. I do not wish to stop for long in so great a cold.

"Our car's stalled," she says. "We're on our way back from Winnipeg. My brother died."

I soften, deferring to death.

She begins to weep. "It's so far. We don't know what to do. We live by Detroit. The car just died. It was my brother's."

I offer consolation, directions. I would help but I must go the other way.

She cries openly. I am the first who cared. The old men are cackling in the other room, full of themselves and their stories.

"His ashes are in the car. God, it's so cold."

Her boyfriend is fumbling with a crumpled paper, trying to find some number. "Where the hell are we?" he blurts. "What town?"

She looks at me, a request in her eyes.

"Shall we get him?" I say.

She looks around. The crudeness of the old men has no reverence. "I just can't leave him out there in this cold."

Her friend is shouting into the receiver. "I can't wait five goddamn hours!"

She nods. We go out. The snow growls and groans beneath our feet. The sky is strange, copper.   The car sits, naked and red, against a drift of snow.

She has no gloves. The key will not work. We bang on a door, trying to break its icy seal. The wind gusts once, cuts our faces with a thousand knives. Our lips crack. She is crying.

"Your tears will freeze," I say. It is not a joke.

In the back I see the urn.

Kent Nerburn

Our breath rages from our mouths. We try other doors. I try to light a match to warm the key. The wind is too strong; the match blows out. My hands freeze. She is staring in the car. "We've got to get him," she screams. Her sobs are frantic, filled with desperation. The cold is lacerating. We bleed pain.

"Just go in," I shout. "I'll get it open."

She runs back to the store. I pull my hat lower. My eyelashes are covered with ice. I kick at the car and curse. Heat is ebbing from me. My legs sting; my toes are numb. The sun hangs lifeless in the frozen sky.

I feel a movement. The seal gives way. With senseless fingers I pry the door from its jamb.

She sees, comes running. Past me, she dives in, throwing aside blankets, maps, fast food wrappers. She grabs the urn and pulls it out, runs back, talking to it like a mother to a foundling child.

I follow, uncertain. Her friend is still shouting into the phone. The old men are still laughing among themselves.

She has huddled on a box. Her back is toward me. She is cradling the urn and speaking softly.

I walk quietly toward the door. What gods live in a land like this, where the cold is so great that we must comfort the dead?

Kent Nerburn

COPSE

It freezes where they abode.
It snows where they abode.
It storms where they abode.
It is cold where they abode.

—Delaware saga

The horizon is a line across a phantom sky. The windblown fields stretch towards infinity. Fragments of cornstalks — brittle shards —stick through the snow and bend and rattle, and the wind is the largest thing, the only thing.

In the distance, copses of trees stand like battlements — isolated, alone, small islands against the prairie sky. On the far horizon, purpling night has started its descent, too soon. There will be no sunset, for there has been no sun, only pale light — weak, and without source. Snowblown, blinding, aluminum, it leaves without event, giving way to dark.

The wind rises up, sensing an ally. It is filled with banshee howls, screams, and distant laughter. Amid the copses single lights go on in farmhouses, miles apart. One, then another, as if in signal.

Fingers of snow drift across the road. "Lose the road, lose your life," the old farmers said, and the snow is drifting, drifting.

Attention takes a fine edge, now. There is no room for error. A man was found last week but a half a mile from his car, frozen. Two weeks they had searched. A gust of wind had revealed his hand, as if clutching, or waving.

It is the swing that stops me. It hangs and twists by a single strand from the arm of a great oak, far back amid a shadowy copse. Behind it, almost lost in darkness, I see the house, abandoned, swaybacked, empty. I should not stop; this is not a night to challenge. But something cries out for witness.

The wind screams in outrage as I step outside. The shadows of the trees grasp at me as I walk.

Movement is hard. My steps punch through the frozen crust. I sink in up to my knees. The wind lashes my face; my chest heaves. Snow burrows in at my ankles, sending waves of pain as the icy wetness cuts the flesh, then begins to freeze. So little time, so little time.

The door is heavy — rude planks covered by torn tarpaper — wedged half-open. Drifts have heaved against it in a frozen wave. In a weathered eave a wasps nest rattles, grey and ragged.

I push hard. The door scrapes open. A froth of snow whisks across the floor. Wolf tracks, or dog, mark a single line to a far corner. Scat covers the floor. Is he here?

Holes have been punched in the walls. The windows are gone. A sink hangs from its plumbing, kicked, perhaps, or hammered. In a corner a stove stands covered with dust and mouse droppings. Its oven door is open, a cry into the night.

On the floor a book is flapping. The pages turn and rustle in the wind, then settle for a moment. I touch it with my foot. It is brittle; pages detach and scatter. One flies up against a wall, where it flutters, like a dying bird, desperate to escape.

Through an empty window I can see the swing, twisting in the winter dark. The wood is grey as bone, and frozen.

That someone thought there was a life to be lived here. That for one

Kent Nerburn

brief moment hands were joined in common effort, and from each hammer blow, each chop of ax, rang out a song of hope.

I see them rise before me. The father, planting shelterbands of trees and planning yields and harvests. The mother, at the stove, cooking dinners, baking bread. And the children, at the swing, called in for dinner from summer play.

Did they have bicycles? Did they ride horses down the road to that next far house among that next far copse, that next small island in this eternal flatness? Did they camp out on warm summer nights, counting the stars and finding messages in an owl's call? Did cicadas sing them to sleep?

Did their father take them aside, in a moment of fine hope, and tell them, "Someday this will all be yours," and mean it as a gift? And did they sit there, listening, thinking in the simple colors of their childhood, how good it would be to someday work this land? Or did they, with each visit to a city or some nearby town, say, "Someday I will leave."

And what of the night that it was decided?

At the table, amid long silences, who was it that said, "Enough, we cannot go on." Was it the woman, wide-eyed and hysterical from too many days alone in this too awful space? Or was she the happy one, hanging clothes in the summer air and gathering her children to her in the evening, while her husband sat vacantly, adding up figures, projecting yields, cursing bankers and God? Did he one day walk in and say, "It is finished. There will be no more."

Or was it something darker that broke their will?

Is there, beneath these snows, a tiny grave, a tragedy too great to be borne? Or did they all, like the pages of the book, simply turn frail, and blow away?

I step among the boards. It is wrong to be here. There is no humility in this defeat, only shame. This is life that wants to be forgotten.

The darkness has risen now, and looms across the land. There is only the great cold, and the shadows, and the wind. Whispers of snow have almost hidden the road. The copse, the house, are disappearing. Darkness is folding them in, like sleep, like death.

I retrace my steps. Already my marks are being erased; they, too, have lost their shape.

I drive in silence, listening to the wind.

In the distance, a church stands lonely in an empty field. It is small, white, boarded up against the winter dark. By its side, a tiny graveyard sits inside a wire fence. There are no tall monuments — such presumption would be unseemly — only a few low stones poking humpbacked through the swirling snow.

Far behind, almost lost in shadow, a single cross stands half buried in the winter night. The wind swirls angrily around it, as if to hide it from my view.

I squint my eyes, as if there is something I have not yet seen. But there is no life anywhere — only the wind, and the dark, and the stark arm of the single cross, protruding, beckoning, like a frozen hand above the drifting snows.

Kent Nerburn

The earth is impatient now.

Small shoots, eager as children, push through the husks

of winter's dying. Their green freshness shrieks.

The older plants, who have spent their

lives above the ground, resist.

They know that winter has not yet

withdrawn in full retreat.

She could rise up and strike them, without mercy,

without warning. Better to withhold, and wait.

There will be time enough; there will be time enough.

Awakenings

All creatures awake and see the light.
Day is here. Day is here, is here.

— Pawnee song

Kent Nerburn

REDEMPTION

My music
Reaches
To the Sky

— Ojibwe song

The fever breaks. The world returns.

How could we have forgotten this sun, this yellow day? Did we not see the birch, the pine? How could colors, and hope, have fled so from our memory? It was not good to live inside a scream.

We step cautiously toward the light. Our legs are unsteady. Outside, the wind still howls in the bones of the trees. The snow still swirls and rises cobra-backed into the frozen day.

But the sun again has life. After three weeks beneath a lifeless sky, we again dare to have a dream greater than survival.

We throw open the windows in the dark rooms of our souls. Light is streaming in. Our spirits turn and rub their eyes. We are moving back toward the surface of our lives. Promise arches over all. We grasp, greedily, at time, and clutch it to us. All tomorrows' mornings stretch before us, languid.

We are no longer islands. We gather, laugh, talk warmly of the time that has passed.

Who outside us knows of days where the cold stole away all the colors, where life was so frozen that every step had an echo?

Let others put names to our darkness, try to shape it into words and pathologies. They have not stared for weeks into a sun that gave no warmth, that gazed upon us with the eye of a corpse, turning our every thought toward death? They have not watched ghost lights drip heatless and molten in a midnight sky, have not heard wolves cry out over frozen waters.

No, this is not illness. We may wish to have been born in the shadow of a mountain, where each day lifted our eyes in something close to awe. Or on the edge of an ocean, where infinity had a softness, and declared itself anew each sunrise. But we were born on the edge of winter, where our lives are marked by absences and fears, and a too intimate knowledge of the ways of death.

But, for now, it has passed. We have been plunged into frozen waters, held until we could not breathe, then lifted up, redeemed. The world assaults us with its beauty. No baptism could be sweeter, no salvation purer.

We raise our hearts in quiet joy and lay down our helpless sticks of fire.

Kent Nerburn

Kent Nerburn

HARBINGER

Behold, my brothers, the spring has come.
The earth has received the embraces of the sun.

— Sitting Bull
Lakota

The earth is slow. It sheds its winter sleep gruffly, like a bear shaking off the night.

Not so the sky. Ever alive to nuance, it waits in harp-string readiness for every harbinger of change.

The first to notice are the birds. Their song has brightness — a music played upon the light. A month ago, if they called at all, it was a lonely sound against the dark. There is excitement now, like a child breathless to reveal a secret.

It is movement we feel. The birdsong moves along the wind. Beneath our feet an ancient rumbling struggles to be heard, with springs and rivulets, and rocks releasing their icy grip upon the ground.

One by one, we free ourselves from the common stillness. Something new will be born.

The animals move with fresh purpose; their actions now meant less to protect than to discover. They raise their heads, paw and claw and chew at tiny objects revealed by the retreating of the snow. They roll and leap and tumble; in their actions lives a sense of play.

Life peers out from every place. The squirrel peers from around a tree. The earth peers through the patchy snow. Where all was one, we once again are many, celebrating the self and the commingling of our growing hopes.

"We have survived. We have survived," is our common song. And none—the bud, the child, the animal at play—can contain our common glee.

Soon our song will break in full. The birds will fly, the dogs will bark. The children will dance across the gurgling ground. Ice will crack and break in concert with the wind. Clouds will race and roll like puppies tumbling in the sky.

We will run through the rain, shrieking, pulling coats above our heads.

This is all we need to know of grace. Even the infants laugh.

Kent Nerburn

RAIN

The rain is all around us . . .
And the summer will be fair to see.

—Tiqua song

It is raining today.

The damp creeps in through the cracks in the walls, and the must of soggy timbers mingles with the dank of soggy air.

My bones rebel. They, too, are filling with moisture, unseen capillaries drinking their fill and turning white brittleness to a boggy grey.

The cat brushes against me. His insistent warmth conjures images of fireplaces and cozy nooks. But today there is no place to hide. The rain has come calling, and it closes down around us like a curtain made of stone.

It is faceless and indifferent, this rain — devoid of the drama of a mountain squall or the power of a prairie thunderhead. It is nourishing the earth's deeper need. We humans can only survive and endure.

I remember such rains in the past, from a winter spent on a small creek in the woods of Oregon. The hills rose tight on either side of the tiny cabin. The days betrayed no passage of time; the nights were dripping darknesses. In the morning we would peer out like animals and search the sky for signs of light. But there was none. We carried on our lives beneath a canopy of gloom.

But in the spring, when the sky broke, the symphony of life was beyond imagining. The earth sprang forth in celebration and embraced us with a flowering joy. There was no need to plant or cultivate. We wandered free amidst a lush harvest.

This rain, too, will bring a lush harvest. Prairie grasses, dormant in their winter brown, will raise their heads and turn to summer green. The fingers of the leafless trees will soften with a fuzzy down. Birdsong will fill the air; phalanxes of wildflowers will march across the hills. The earth will be alive with chirps and buzzing sounds.

But for now, the rain covers all, testing our capacity to wait.

It is good to know such rain. It calls us to examine the landscape of our hearts. Distances are muted and the sounds plunge down from heaven. We are enclosed — at once denied the joy of distant vistas and protected from the intrusions of unseen events.

It is now that we truly know ourselves as creatures of the earth. The heavens in their relentless indifference are pounding down upon us with a purpose that transcends our time and scale.

I settle back and stare out through the window's tearful blinded eye.

The cat winds slowly around my leg, then settles in a corner, closing in upon himself. His muffled breathing rises and falls — rhythmic, eternal, like the pounding of a distant surf.

Kent Nerburn

Kent Nerburn

OFFERING

We are like birds with a broken wing
My heart is cold within me
My eyes are growing dim
I am old

— Plenty Coups
Crow chief

The old woman sits with a sweater over her shoulders. Her cloudy eyes are huge behind thick glasses.

From her window we can see the great lake breaking up. Chunks of ice are being pushed against the shore by the north wind, where they are piling into great mounds of jagged blue wreckage.

The children sit at her feet, polite, quiet, attentive.

"In the spring of the year," she is saying, "after the ice melted away from the lake, my grandmother would tell my mother to get a young popple tree and make some sticks about five inches long, then peel off the bark, and tie them together in a roll about a yard long, with two strings.

"Then she would tie a piece of everybody's clothing that belongs to our household, then a small bundle of tobacco, a medium-sized rock, and a live little black puppy, and put it in the water. It was to appease the gods of the lake so we wouldn't drown."

The children glance at each other. The old woman smiles and reaches for them. They draw back from her; she has breath like death.

She talks on. Her voice is singsong; the Ojibwe rhythms can be heard underneath.

"In the summer we used to play on the sand where it slopes to the shore from the hills. We would roll down the hills with our dresses on, then play in the water, then go rolling down again. Then mother would call us and say, 'There's gods in there. They'll come and snatch you and take you in further.'"

The children inch closer to me. One little girl pushes against my leg and grabs my hand. Outside the great ice sheets thunder and groan.

"One time God got mad at the people on the earth. They were so bad that he sent a flood and drowned them all. We got our water from the lake out there, then. In the spring, it was pretty deep and the water looked grey and gloomy. I just got scared, and I thought, 'Maybe God will get mad at us again, and drown us.'"

The little girl stares up at me. Her eyes are dark, pleading. I put my fingers to my lips: "A little longer." The woman has been kind enough to share her stories.

She tells them of being sent out in storms to place tobacco beneath trees to ward off the thunder gods, of old men in the forest who would get you and make you their wife if you wandered too far from your mother.

She moves her eyes, her breath, toward them. "Two men came to the boarding school when I was ten years old. I didn't understand English much, then. They gave them permission to have Sunday school and an evening song service. I didn't know what they were talking about. But a strange thing happened to me. They gave us these little cards with pictures on them, and I was dreaming, seeing these cards floating by in the sky. Especially one picture of a man kneeling by a huge rock with his eyes lifted toward heaven and his folded hands on the rock.

"They were always talking about hell, and that got me scared. Seems like all my years of life, Grandma was scaring me with her gods. Now, here

Kent Nerburn

was another god I got to be scared of."

The woman bares her teeth and smiles. "Grandfather must have heard about these missionaries and he talked to me. 'My girl, I hear there's two men at that school who teach Christian. My girl, don't listen to them. That's white man's religion they're talking about. We Indians can go to heaven. God has prepared a different place for us to go when we die.'"

She is coming to an end. She holds out her hands, like tree branches, like bones. "Now listen to me. There's danger out there, and getting worse. Life is like that. Full of dangers. The evils get us. We get addicted, hooked, and we meet death. It's all over with."

She lifts herself up and shuffles toward the kitchen. Her glasses glint like the ice sheets on the lake.

"I've got something for you," she says, and we hear the oven door creak and fall open.

The little girl releases my hand. Outside, the lake breathes steam into the fading sky. The ice heaves and sighs and pushes further onto the shore.

I take my son to the edge of our lake, give him instructions. I do not send him to get strips of clothing or to cut saplings of popple. I do not mention puppies. I do not even tell him of the great flood, and have him look into greying waters with a deeper fear. There are no old men waiting in the woods for him. All is chipmunks, and bears with names, and lessons.

He listens politely — a good boy — and goes off, untroubled, to play.

Do the gods cease to exist when no one believes in them? Do they pack up and move on, while others take over the rent and set up housekeeping in our souls?

Last summer three boys drowned on the lake outside the old woman's house. Their bodies were found, days later, washed up on shore. The whole community was in shock. They knew the lake so well, it was said, and they were all such strong swimmers. No one could understand.

The elders attended the funeral and said nothing.

What cautions should I give my son as he ventures onto the waters? Should I be teaching him to recite, "Peace, be still," or to call out to Jesus if the waves increase, to await the hand that will lift him up? Or should I be bringing him solemnly to the shore to stare into a puppy's terrified eyes as I cast it, weighted down with stones, into the murky waters?

I am not Abraham. I do not want to risk my son.

The old woman is returning. We can hear her feet moving across the floor. She comes through the door carrying a plate of cookies. The children rush for them greedily, thankful to be free from her tales.

She looks at me and nods. I take one, and smile — I do not wish to be impolite — and slip it in my pocket.

Later, as we are leaving, when I am sure no one is watching, I walk to the shore and cast it, like a wafer, upon the moaning, darkening waters.

Kent Nerburn

Kent Nerburn

FLOOD

Weep, my unfortunate people,
For the waters will overwhelm the land.

— Pima song

The water, now, is everywhere.

The snows have melted and are in retreat. The sounds of drippings and rushings fill the night — without direction, without source. We lie in our beds and listen.

From far away the reports have come, of the Crow, the Red, and a host of nameless creeks and rivers that have breached their banks. Already small towns have disappeared — Warren, Hallock — names unknown except in times of crisis or disaster.

Pictures come to us of families on the roofs of old frame houses, of cattle stranded on islands formed from farmers' fields.

Grim men, with a holy faith in God and hard labor, work under spotlights late into the night, filling sandbags, passing them from hand to hand.

They awake in the morning to measure their losses.

I stand at the edge of our lake, calculating run offs, making hopeless efforts at conversions of inches of ice into volume of water. The marks from the day before, the sticks stuck into the bank at high water, have disappeared.

Above me, the birds perch silently in the trees. They know, from their circling vantage, that this land is but the remnant of the glacier; our roads and settlements no more than tiny islands in this fading memory of an inland sea.

Night falls. The waters continue to rise. They move, dark and reptilian, among the trees, soundlessly, like a thief in a house at night.

In the darkness we hear the sounds of frogs and crawling things. Large animals crash through the brush in retreat.

Morning. Word is passed. The water has taken the road.

For days we have watched the fields on either side disappear beneath the brooding waters until they have become, now, shapeless lakes. We have ridden thankfully, nervously, upon the gravel hump that passes between them, higher by inches than the water that surrounds us.

Now, a finger of water has cut across, and the road, and all illusion of control, have disappeared.

I run down to see. The water is rushing across like an army that has breached a wall — soldiers run amok in a foreign land, without rules, without remorse.

I can wait no longer. I am no Noah, casting my hope upon the waters and offering up a dove. I must part the sea.

Down to the lake. My feet are deep within it now. The water broods around my legs, ominous, like a nest of snakes.

There must be a key. I am human. I have a mind. I can find it.

Through the waters, knee deep, frozen, pushing chunks of ice.

There are rules: gravity, direction, flow.

I will find it.

I thrash to the channel where the waters flow out into another lake. Ahead of me I see it — woven, tangled, crafted — a dam, a beaver's plaything, blocking the outlet. I marvel at its chaotic majesty. I could not block this flow

Kent Nerburn

with sticks and wattle. What divine skill of instinct gave him this knowledge?

I set about its destruction. My thighs are frozen. I can no longer feel my feet.

I push through the waters with hopefulness and rage. I have discovered the key, the Rosetta Stone. With my ax I will unlock the secret.

The water will flow. The lake will go down.

I will stand and watch the torrent rush into the next creek and the next bay and the next lake until it finds its way to the great river and back into the land.

It will release it and I will make no apologies to beavers or to God.

An ax, a shovel, a pick, chopping. The waters curling at my thighs, frigid.

I pull. Branches come loose, turn vertical, and shoot through. A trickle, then a flow.

Still, I cannot break it free. The great force cannot be released.

I stare into the murky depths, as clear as ice, as green as death.

There, far beneath the surface, it lies: a single pole as thick as my arm, gnawed pencil-sharp on each end, longer by inches than the opening it spans. Weeds and sticks are woven around it, forming a barrier to the full force of the water's passage.

The mason's keystone. The carpenter's roof beam.

With frantic urgency I chop at it with the ax, pull at it. It fights its way back into position. The water is pushing me hard, threatening to topple me. There is no feeling left. Ice chunks crash against me, flow by.

How did he know? What measure did he use? Another foot longer and it would not have fit. Another foot shorter and it would not have spanned. What geometry? What divine and infernal calculus? I rage at his cleverness.

I am cursing, shouting, bellowing against the waters. Grunts, laughter — punctuations of my successes and failures as the trees and the branches break.

The dam gives, fragments, rushes away. I howl and snort.

Then, behind me, I sense it. A presence, watching. The beaver, perhaps? Come to bear witness to the destruction of his labors?

I tense. Does God build vengeance into such a creature?

I turn, the ax at the ready. But it is only a small boy sitting quietly on the bank, wide-eyed, fascinated.

"Beaver," I say. "Blocked the outlet."

But the boy is gone. Discovered, or perhaps frightened by my upraised ax, he has disappeared back into the woods. I can hear him thrashing through the underbrush.

I gather my tools and claw my way up the bank. The water is flowing freely now. I can hear it rushing through the outlet.

I call out for the boy once more. I want to show him, to recount the struggle. But he will not answer.

I turn to survey my handiwork. Ice and sticks are rushing through the opening. The lake is going down.

But the ax feels clumsy in my hand, and I feel no sense of victory, only some vague sense of violation and the sting of embarrassment at being denied the right of explanation.

Kent Nerburn

GOOD FRIDAY

At the end of the earth
The sky will weep.

-Fox wailing song

The morning comes, vesper calm and lavender, over still waters. She separates herself from night and stretches pink-limbed and languid across the sky.

The earth, dark animal, exhales. Her children move.

We are rising to take back the day.

But there is strangeness in this dawn — a silence, too strong, like a thousand water birds ascending without sound.

We search the heavens for a sign.

Nine a.m. There has been no movement. The trees will not whisper. Far above us, the moon retreats silently, like memory.

Ten a.m. The animals are confused. They rush out, move briskly, then retreat. The air is nervous, heavy, like sweat.

Noon, and no release. We sit in half light. The edges of the curtains rustle.

Two p.m. The sky darkens. Clouds move like armies, silent, with intent.

Three p.m. The light is dying. The earth holds its breath. The sky turns the yellow of an animal's eye. Where is the lamb to break this seal?

Three fifteen. Dragon's eyes flash from beyond the horizon. The trees bow their heads. The storm rushes down upon us with the quality of nightmare.

We hear the footsteps of giants, and we apologize for our dreams.

We hear the footsteps of giants, and we apologize for our dreams.

I sit, uneasy, behind walls that bend and groan. Two by fours, right angles, offer fragile harbor.

I would light a candle, intone a chant, if I knew what to do. Make a mark in blood upon the door. But my hands are bound; my voice is mute.

The only mysteries now are life and death, and even they are being laid open on a table. Love is reduced to instinct; God is diminished to idea. Wind is nothing more than a noun, a house from which all life has fled.

If it were mine to do, there would be no more such entombments of meaning inside bloodless structures. No noun could stand alone, devoid of intention. Each tree would have a name, each wind would have a voice.

I would take those words already dead, and burn them on a great pyre. I would summon this wind, and dance blindly as it raised the flames, consuming all the frail houses of our understanding.

It would be the self that would burn, that brittle husk. My point of view would shrivel, curl, and disappear. And when the fire died, all would come alive in the darkness.

And into that great silence I would cast this prayer:
Let me know this wind again as the breath of God.
Let me feel it as angry.
Let the fear of its coming, and the joy of its relenting,
    have me carving effigies and piling stones upon a hill.
Let me genuflect in silence as the rocks call out each other's names.

Kent Nerburn

Kent Nerburn

WIND

How the wind whistles now. . .
High through the night it flies,
Still hunting the prey that runs.

— Iroquois chant of darkness

She rises now, insane, from the northwest, upon her haunches. We should have prepared, made supplication. But we were dancing, and held in the fullness of time. Now we must pay tribute, and we do not know the coin.

Set a sentinel on the shoulder of the gods. Point him there, toward the Canadian prairies, to the distant arctic. Have him set his eyes along the great flyway of the winds to warn us of days like this.

It is getting dangerous now. Trees bend too far. Windows rattle; doors knock on their hinges. The sky is a holocaust of noise.

When this is over, something will be changed. Somewhere, in the petty movements of our day, we will come upon a wreckage.

I move to the corner of the house. This is the stuff of childhood nightmare. Tigers, flocks of birds to peck out our eyes, forces coming from all directions, merciless. A great wolf to blow the house down.

In my youth, I knew such dreams as this. I would hide and huddle in the corner of my mind, then wake in a sweat, turn on lights, and breathe deeply until my heart would settle.

Now I am older. I shape my understanding into boxes, contain it in words and concepts. Dreams can still bring terror, but I am quick to define their edges and to go about my days.

But this is no dream. This is wind that wants to rip something apart.

The long dark is over; the days are full of light.

There is gentleness now, of soft twilights,

lambent dawns.

Waters kiss at the shores.

The air is filled with blossom fragrance.

The birds speak in rapid cadence, scolding,

warning, singing out in simple joy.

At water's edge the deer come down to drink.

Popple turn their leaves to the wind, and the aspen

whisper matins to the dawn.

We turn our eyes toward the heavens.

For these brief moments we are held in the

hands of gentler gods.

Solaces

Just over there the dawn is coming
Now I hear soft laughter

— Papago song

─── (LEGACY) ───

Hark, the trees, whispering
Bend their old bodies low.

— Iroquois chant

I take my walk down to the shore. Shadows of the clouds move like thoughts across the waters. The lake rolls gently, kitten soft.

I pick up a stone — round, washed, ancient — and cast it upon the waters. It hits, dark and hollow; the rings spread out like memories.

Far in the distance a heron surges upward, an ungainly question mark seeking flight.

Before me I see the pine. He stands beside the shore — quiet, stolid, beckoning. I accept his offer, take the pleasure of his rest.

I know him well. We have sat together often.

He is virtuous, unwavering, singular in his devotion to the sky. Through the years the wind has bent him slightly; he leans now toward the south, an act of accommodation more than yearning.

Each year I sense a growing weariness within him. His branches droop; he no longer raises green shoots in celebration to the sun. He is surrounded now by birch, young children excited by the day. They send forth their buds without caution at the first sign of warmth. They know nothing of his silent rectitude, his severe and holy devotion.

I watch him more closely now. He is old, brittle. A storm could snap him. I listen as he leans and groans. But when the wind has passed he spreads his arms to dance an old man's dance against the breeze.

I am his only friend now. Children no longer play beneath his branches. He is too dark; his needles are too sharp. They would rather climb the birch, the aspen; smell the apple and the plum. They run to him only when sticks are needed for a fire. His dead limbs snap like fingers, burst quickly into flame.

"You should cut it down," the neighbor says. "It could fall on your house."

But I will not. I know his private courage. And my father sat beneath him once, though he was old, and could remember nothing.

Kent Nerburn

Kent Nerburn

BIRTHRIGHT

Now this is the day.
Our child,
Into the daylight
You will go out standing.

— Zuni presentation song

I am in shadow, behind. He does not see. He kneels at water's edge, picks feathers, lifts stones. He sings as he plays. His world is liquid, private, deep.

Who is this child of mine who finds in stones a song? What morning grace so gently lifts his spirit?

He moves, a feather in each hand, waves his arms in mimicked flight. A songbird, an eagle, a young Icarus unmindful of the sun.

I want him to keep this brightness, to be a child of light, a lion, a bringer of song. Yet in his eyes I see that distance, that hawk circling on November's wind.

Is this his birthright? Is this what must be passed?

A child should have his grasping at the sunbeams, and his giggling laughters, puppy-tousled tumblings, days full of joyousness and grace. His sadnesses should be personal, tragic, ephemeral and loud. Distant darknesses have no place in childhood, even if they run in the blood.

And so I have come to water's edge, where sunrise and sunset paint in liquid shimmerings. Here the shadows move with dancers' grace, and evanescence keeps the deeper darknesses at bay.

Come, child, let me lift you. Let me raise you up and point for you the colors and the movements, the ever-renewing majesty of sunsets, full moons, and dawns.

Look not at me, but at where I point. For I have come to know and love these fragile days. My childhood questionings, my youthful ragings, where I tossed my ragdoll faith toward the dark eternity only to see it fall, rumpled, back to earth — those are gone. I now caress the mornings with a lover's touch. The sunsets come back to me with the faithfulness of friendship.

Come, share these with me. Hear the windsong, birdsong, waters lapping at the shore.

We live beneath a father's sky that changes wonder to uncertainty. No wind blows warm that does not echo of a colder day. No sunlight lives that does not have the hint of shadow.

These gentle sounds will give you balm. They will quiet the blood that courses through us darker than a river.

Come, come, my son.

Listen closely. Caress the stones. Feel the protection of the trees.

This is our baptism, yours and mine. The lullaby of waters.

Above this land stars pivot on a point of love.

Kent Nerburn

Kent Nerburn

SANCTUS

I am sitting close to the sunrise now, near to the holy.

I do not do this often.

We wake only after the bells, after the cock has crowed three times. We know almost nothing of the dawn, of the first movements, unsteady, on newborn feet. And when we do, they too often pass unnoticed, coming forth against our leaving, as we move towards our beds and sleep, full vessels, sated, blind and weary from the night.

Such a time as this requires silence of the heart. We must lay out a blanket for the gods and leave an offering, untouched, that can be carried off by hummingbirds. No bloody rams, no virgins, nothing that contains the taint and stain of sacrifice. We know too well what we are, what we have become.

If I could place an infant's breath before this sky, that is what I would do. If I could fly, and dedicate my weightlessness, or sing in a voice that disappeared, unheard, into the wind, these are the offerings I would make. A holy shroud, with the echo of a savior.

It is rising now. Orange, new, eternal, a perfect circle over still waters, and I am crazy with the light.

I shall vanish

and be no more.

But the land I now roam

shall remain

and shall not change.

— Omaha warrior song